SUFFOLK
TRAVEL GUIDE 2024

Exploring the Hidden Gems of Suffolk's Countryside

Ramiro Hassan

COPYRIGHT © 2024 BY RAMIRO HASSAN

No portion of this book may be copied, distributed, or transmitted in any way without the publisher's prior written consent; the only exceptions are brief quotes included in critical reviews and certain other non-commercial uses allowed by copyright law. This includes photocopying, recording, and other electronic or mechanical methods.

TABLE OF CONTENTS

CHAPTER ONE: INTRODUCTION

CHAPTER TWO: GETTING TO SUFFOLK

CHAPTER THREE: SUFFOLK'S ICONIC LANDMARKS

CHAPTER FOUR: OUTDOOR ACTIVITIES AND NATURE

CHAPTER FIVE: SUFFOLK'S COASTAL ATTRACTIONS

CHAPTER SIX: ARTS AND CULTURE IN SUFFOLK

CHAPTER SEVEN: FOOD AND DRINK

CHAPTER EIGHT: SHOPPING AND LOCAL PRODUCTS

CHAPTER NINE: ACCOMMODATION IN SUFFOLK

CHAPTER TEN: CONCLUSION

CHAPTER ONE: INTRODUCTION

The Magic of Suffolk

Situated on England's east coast, the county of Suffolk is renowned for its serene beach towns, historical sites, and scenic scenery. Visitors may experience a distinctive fusion of natural beauty and ancient history in Suffolk, which has broad beaches, rolling farmland, and an abundance of cultural sites.

East Anglia, which includes Suffolk, has a rich history that dates back to the Anglo-Saxon era. It has had a major impact on how England's political and cultural environment has developed. Suffolk is a popular tourist destination for a variety of interests, including history fans, nature lovers, foodies, and art connoisseurs. It is the perfect location for anybody looking for a tranquil escape or an exploration of England's interesting history because of its varied attractions and peaceful atmosphere.

Suffolk's inherent appeal, plethora of events, and new attractions will make it a popular tourist destination in 2024. Suffolk has something for everyone, regardless of whether you're thinking of taking a long weekend trip or a longer one.

Why Visit Suffolk in 2024?
Suffolk is a location where modernity and history collide, and the variety of experiences it provides is a testament to its distinct personality. Here are some reasons to think about going to Suffolk in 2024:

1. Magnificent Sceneries and Outdoor Occupations
Some of England's most exquisite scenery may be found in Suffolk, where wide coasts, verdant woodlands, and rolling hills coexist. Hiking,

cycling, and birding are made possible by the breathtaking scenery of the Dedham Vale AONB and the Suffolk Coast and Heaths Area of Outstanding Natural Beauty (AONB). Numerous nature reserves can be found throughout the county, such as RSPB Minsmere, which is well-known for its wide variety of bird species and breathtaking landscape.

2. A Wealthy Heritage and History
The many historic structures and landmarks in Suffolk attest to its historical importance. Among the most well-known are Sutton Hoo, Orford Castle, and Framlingham Castle. For those who like history, Sutton Hoo is a must-see. Anglo-Saxon ship burial remains from antiquity may be found there, offering priceless insights into the early Middle Ages. Suffolk's rich history is further enhanced by the county's many ancient churches and historic homes, such as Ickworth House.

3. A Dynamic Cultural Environment

Suffolk has a thriving and diversified cultural scene, with festivals and events held all year round. Composer Benjamin Britten established the famed Aldeburgh Festival, which draws world-class musicians and spectators from all over the world. In addition, the county is home to a number of literary gatherings, theatrical productions, and arts and crafts fairs, giving guests plenty of chances to fully engage with Suffolk's cultural scene.

4. Adorable Seaside Villages and Towns

The coastline of Suffolk is lined with quaint beach villages and towns, each with a distinct personality. Popular vacation spots include Dunwich, Southwold, and Aldeburgh because of their laid-back vibes and gorgeous surroundings. There are many things to do in these cities, such as dining at neighborhood eateries serving fresh seafood or strolling down charming streets dotted with small stores and cafés. While Aldeburgh is well-known for its pebble beach and Benjamin Britten links, Southwold is particularly well-known for its magnificent pier and Adnams Brewery.

5. Snacking Pleasures

The culinary scene in Suffolk offers a delicious mix of modern and classic dishes. The county is well-known for its products that are supplied locally, especially the cheese, fresh fish, and pig from Suffolk. Dining options for visitors include quaint cafés, quaint taverns, and award-winning restaurants. The Suffolk Food Hall, which is close to Ipswich, is a wonderful location to try regional cuisine and buy handcrafted goods. Furthermore, the county has a number of food festivals and farmers' markets all year round, affording a special chance to sample the finest that Suffolk has to offer in terms of cuisine.

6. Attractions Suitable for Families

With a range of family-friendly sites and activities, Suffolk is a great place to visit. The county has many family-friendly attractions, such as Easton Farm Park, Jimmy's Farm and Wildlife Park, and Africa Alive! Wildlife Park. Youngsters will also take pleasure in touring Felixstowe's Landguard Fort and the Suffolk Owl Sanctuary, which provide entertaining and instructive experiences.

7. Easily Reachable and Welcome

Suffolk is a great place for both domestic and foreign visitors since it's conveniently located near London and other important English cities. A pleasant and restful vacation is facilitated by the warm attitude of the county and its amiable residents. There are lodging alternatives in Suffolk to fit every taste and budget, from little bed & breakfasts to opulent hotels.

8. Distinctive Retail Experiences

Suffolk provides a distinctive retail experience, emphasizing individual stores and regional craftspeople. Discover unique products and keepsakes by perusing boutiques, antique stores, and artisan fairs. Particularly well-known for their shopping areas are the towns of Bury St. Edmunds, Woodbridge, and Lavenham, where tourists may purchase everything from antique apparel to handcrafted jewelry.

9. Ecotourism

Suffolk is dedicated to environmentally friendly travel, working to preserve its natural surroundings and uplift the community. Numerous tourist destinations and lodging options in the county encourage sustainable practices and minimize their carbon impact. Because of its emphasis on sustainability, Suffolk appeals to tourists who care about the environment.

10. All-year Appeal

With something to offer every season of the year, Suffolk is a year-round destination. The landscape comes alive in the spring with colorful vegetation and blossoming flowers. Autumn brings gorgeous foliage and harvest festivities, while summer is ideal for outdoor activities and beach trips. Winter offers a warm ambiance with fun-filled markets and activities. Suffolk guarantees a remarkable experience whenever you come.

In summary

Visitors are enthralled by Suffolk County's natural beauty, extensive history, and lively culture. In 2024, tourists will find it to be an enticing destination due to its variety of activities, friendly attitude, and dedication to sustainability. Suffolk offers a variety of activities, including historical site exploration, outdoor recreation, sampling regional food, and artistic immersion. Make travel plans to Suffolk in 2024 and experience the allure of this charming English county.

CHAPTER TWO: GETTING TO SUFFOLK

Transportation Options

Via Train

By rail is one of the easiest methods to get to Suffolk. The county benefits from excellent access to the UK's railway network, which connects it to important cities like Norwich, Cambridge, and London. The Great Eastern Main route, which runs from London Liverpool Street to Norwich, is the main railway route that serves Suffolk.

From London: Liverpool Street Station in London is the departure point for trains to Suffolk. Several Suffolk towns, such as Ipswich, Bury St. Edmunds, and Lowestoft, are reachable by direct rail. It usually takes one hour and fifteen minutes to go from London to Ipswich and one hour and forty-five minutes to get to Bury St. Edmunds. It should take around two hours and thirty minutes to get to Lowestoft.

From Cambridge: Direct trains run to Ipswich and Bury St. Edmunds from Cambridge. It takes roughly forty minutes to go from Cambridge to Bury St. Edmunds and one hour and twenty minutes to get to Ipswich.

From Norwich: There are direct trains from Norwich to a number of Suffolk locations, such as Lowestoft and Ipswich. It takes around forty minutes to go from Norwich to Ipswich and fifty minutes to get to Lowestoft.

It's essential to purchase tickets in advance for train travel in order to get the best deals and steer clear of last-minute rushes. To get timetables and make reservations, you may utilize National Rail and Greater Anglia.

Via Automobile

You may be flexible and take your time exploring the area when you drive to Suffolk. Major highways from London and other places link the county effectively to the UK road network.

From London: The A12 highway, which travels via Ipswich and other Suffolk towns on its way to Great Yarmouth, is the most popular route from London to Suffolk. Travelers traveling from London or other areas of the UK will find it straightforward to reach the A12 from the M25 highway.

From Cambridge: The A14 highway, which links Cambridge to Ipswich and other areas of Suffolk, is accessible if you are traveling by car. It is also accessible from other areas via the A14, which connects to the M11 motorway.

From Norwich: The main road to Suffolk, which leads to Ipswich and other locations, is the A140 for travelers from Norwich.

Discovering Suffolk's rural regions and seaside villages by car gives you access to places that are often inaccessible by public transit. But keep in mind that some of Suffolk's roads, particularly those in rural regions, may be twisting and narrow. In certain areas, be ready for reduced driving speeds.

Via coach and bus

Bus and coach services provide a reasonably priced means of transportation to Suffolk, especially for those on a tight budget. Long-distance coach services from National Express link Suffolk with London and other important UK cities.

From London: Ipswich and Bury St. Edmunds are served by National Express coaches departing from London Victoria Coach Station. By bus, the trip takes roughly two hours and thirty minutes from London to Ipswich and three hours to Bury St. Edmunds.

From Cambridge: Although less common, coach services are nevertheless offered from Cambridge to Suffolk. There are links to Ipswich and Bury St. Edmunds, with travel times varying based on the route.

From Norwich: Regional companies often provide bus and coach services from Norwich to Suffolk, with links to Ipswich and other places. For the most up-to-date information, see your local bus schedule.

Budget travelers might consider bus and coach travel since it is often less expensive than traveling by rail or automobile. But be advised that, compared to rail services, travel durations may be longer and timetables may be less frequent.

Through Air

Although there isn't a large airport in Suffolk, you may travel to one in the area and then continue your trip by bus, rail, or automobile.

Stansted Airport: About an hour's drive from Ipswich, London Stansted Airport is the closest major airport to Suffolk. You may drive or take the rail from Stansted to Cambridge, from where you can go to Suffolk. Alternatively, you may drive straight to your destination in Suffolk by renting a vehicle from Stansted Airport.

Norwich Airport: For those arriving by air, there is also Norwich Airport, which is situated in Norfolk. You may drive or take the rail from Norwich to Suffolk.

By Water

If you are coming from Europe, you may want to consider crossing the English Channel by ferry to the UK and then driving or taking the train to Suffolk.

Harwich International Port: This port is situated in Essex, not far from the border with Suffolk. Travelers from Europe have an alternative, as ferries from the Hook of Holland in the Netherlands dock in Harwich. You may drive or take the rail from Harwich to Ipswich and other locations in Suffolk.

By bicycle
Suffolk has a network of bike trails and beautiful routes for cyclists. Cycling from nearby counties to Suffolk allows you to see the county's rural and coastal regions at your own leisure. Numerous routes on the National Cycle Network pass through Suffolk, offering a distinctive perspective on the region.

Navigating Suffolk

Once you're in Suffolk, you may explore the county's many attractions and move about using a variety of transportation choices.

Via Automobile

One of the most adaptable methods to go about Suffolk is by car, which lets you see the countryside, coastal towns, and other attractions at your own speed. Major towns and villages in Suffolk are connected by a network of highways that offers picturesque journeys through the rural areas.

Renting a vehicle: If you didn't travel by vehicle, there are many places in Suffolk where you may hire one, including Ipswich, Lowestoft, and Bury St. Edmunds. Several major vehicle rental companies have outlets around the county, including Hertz, Enterprise, and Avis.

Parking: Keep in mind that there may be parking restrictions in certain places in Suffolk while driving, particularly in town centers and well-known tourist destinations. Although there are often public parking lots and on-street parking available, it's a good idea to verify parking laws and pay for parking when necessary.

Driving Advice: Exercise care while driving on Suffolk's rural roads since they may be twisting and narrow. In these locations, expect to drive at a slower pace and be cautious around agricultural equipment and bicyclists. Furthermore, keep an eye out for animals, including deer, that could cross roadways in rural regions.

Via Train
In Suffolk, the rail provides a practical means of transportation between larger towns. Greater Anglia connects Ipswich, Lowestoft, Bury St.

Edmunds, and other locations with rail services operating across the county.

Train timetables: Although Suffolk's train services are usually dependable, it's a good idea to check timetables ahead of time so you can arrange your trip. To locate train times and make reservations, visit the Greater Anglia website or applications like National Rail.

Train Stations: Ipswich is the primary center for Suffolk's network of train stations. Bury St. Edmunds, Lowestoft, Stowmarket, and Sudbury are among the other stations. You may connect to other UK towns and regions from these stations.

Via Bus

Buses are an economical means of transportation within Suffolk, enabling one to visit smaller towns and villages that may not be reachable by rail. The county is served by a number of regional bus operators, including First Eastern Counties and Stephensons of Essex.

Bus lines: Suffolk's bus lines link smaller villages and coastal regions with larger towns like Ipswich and Bury St. Edmunds. To plan your trip, utilize transit apps or the websites of local bus operators to check the timetable.

Bus Fares: In Suffolk, bus travel is often inexpensive, making it a cost-effective mode of transportation. For regular passengers, several bus operators provide day passes or multi-journey tickets, which might result in significant savings.

By bicycle

Riding a bicycle is a popular way to see Suffolk, particularly the coastal and rural areas. The county is home to a network of roads and bike lanes that link cities and villages.

Cycle Routes: There are a number of beautiful cycling routes in Suffolk that are part of the National Cycle Network. Among the notable roads are Route 51, which links Ipswich and Bury St. Edmunds, and Route 1, which hugs the Suffolk coast.

Cycle-Friendly Towns: With designated bike lanes and spaces for bicycle parking, many Suffolk towns are bike-friendly. Particularly friendly to cyclists, Ipswich and Bury St. Edmunds have a variety of bicycle facilities.

Renting a Bicycle: If you don't possess a bicycle, you may hire one at Southwold, Ipswich, and Aldeburgh, among other places in Suffolk. Road bikes, mountain bikes, and electric bikes are just a few of the bicycles that are usually available for hire at bike rental stores.

On Foot

A wonderful way to take in the county's natural beauty and historic monuments is to explore Suffolk on foot. There are many pathways and walking routes in Suffolk that go through the countryside, through woodlands, and along the shore.

Walking Trails: The Stour Valley Path, which follows the River Stour through the Dedham Vale Area of Outstanding Natural Beauty, and the Suffolk Coast Path, which stretches down the coast from Felixstowe to Lowestoft, are two of the most well-known walking trails in Suffolk. These routes provide breathtaking vistas and an opportunity to discover Suffolk's topography.

Historic Sites: It's better to tour a lot of Suffolk's historic sites on foot. Historic centers with cobblestone lanes and medieval structures may be found in towns like Lavenham and Bury St. Edmunds. On foot, you may also explore ancient homes and gardens, including Sutton Hoo and Ickworth House.

Footpaths: Suffolk has a vast network of bridleways and public footpaths that let you explore rural regions and get in touch with the natural world. When utilizing these trails, be mindful to respect private property and adhere to local restrictions.

In summary

There is a wide variety of transportation available in Suffolk to travel to and around the county. All types of travelers will find something to enjoy in Suffolk, whether they are more comfortable using the rail or bus, having more freedom while driving, or taking their time when cycling or strolling. You can get the most out of your trip to this beautiful and historic county by making advance plans and selecting the best mode of transportation for your requirements.

CHAPTER THREE: SUFFOLK'S ICONIC LANDMARKS

A Guide to Must-See Locations

1. The Hoosier

One of the most important archaeological sites in England is Sutton Hoo. This location, which is close to Woodbridge, is well-known for its Anglo-Saxon ship burial, which is thought to be the last resting place of a 7th-century monarch or noble. Numerous relics from the burial, including a helmet, weapons, and gold jewelry, are now kept at the British Museum.

In addition to learning about the excavation process and seeing reconstructions of some of the most significant artifacts, visitors may tour the burial mounds. There is a visitor center at Sutton Hoo that offers background and details on the historical importance of the location.

2. The Castle in Framlingham
Situated in the town of Framlingham lies a beautiful medieval stronghold known as Framlingham Castle. Constructed in the latter part of the 12th century, the castle has a striking thirteen-turret curtain wall. During the Tudor period, it was crucial, as Mary I garnered support here before her triumphant ascension to the English throne.

The castle's wall walk, which offers sweeping views of the surrounding landscape, is accessible to visitors. A comprehensive exhibition describing the castle's history and importance in English history is also available.

3. The Aldeburgh

Aldeburgh is a quaint seaside town renowned for its shingle beach and artistic legacy. Once a thriving hub for shipbuilding and fishing, it is now a well-liked vacation spot for tourists looking for a typical English beach experience.

Benjamin Britten, the composer who established the yearly Aldeburgh Festival, which draws performers and spectators from all over the world, has a special connection to the town. Alongside the famous Scallop sculpture by Maggi Hambling, which pays homage to Britten, Aldeburgh is home to the historic Moot Hall, a Tudor structure that was formerly used as a courthouse.

4. The Lavenham

Lavenham is a stunningly preserved medieval village distinguished by its cobblestone streets and half-timbered houses. Lavenham's wealth is evident in its architecture; the town was once among the richest in England in the fifteenth century as a result of the wool trade.

Throughout the ages, the Guildhall of Corpus Christi, a remarkable timber-framed structure owned by the National Trust, has functioned as an almshouse, workhouse, and guildhall. Another noteworthy site is St. Peter and St. Paul's Church, which has an imposing tower and elaborate stonework.

5. The Southwold

Another charming seaside town with a lively vibe is Southwold. It has a sandy beach bordered by vibrant beach huts, as well as a traditional pier with rides and a café. Southwold is noted for its lighthouse, which has been guiding sailors along the coast since 1887.

The town is also famed for its brewery, Adnams, which has been brewing beer in Southwold since the 19th century. Visitors may take a tour of the brewery to learn about the brewing process and taste some of the products.

Exploring Suffolk's Historical Sites

1. Bury St. Edmunds

Bury St. Edmunds is an ancient market town with a strong ecclesiastical past. It is named for St. Edmund, the patron saint of England before St. George, whose shrine was placed in the town's monastery. The remains of Bury St. Edmunds Abbey are a prominent attraction, reflecting the magnitude and magnificence of the medieval edifice.

St. Edmundsbury Cathedral, close to the abbey remains, is a remarkable example of Gothic Revival architecture. It was constructed in the early 21st century, making it one of the newest cathedrals in the nation. Visitors may tour the cathedral's interior, which contains beautiful stained glass windows and a spectacular ceiling.

Bury St. Edmunds also contains the famous Angel Hotel, which has entertained prominent visitors like Charles Dickens. The town's market square is teeming with activity, and tourists may enjoy the various stores, cafés, and restaurants in the neighborhood.

2. Orford Castle

Orford Castle is a remarkable historical landmark situated in the community of Orford. The castle's central keep, which was constructed in the twelfth century by King Henry II, has been beautifully maintained. With a spiral staircase that leads to the roof and a distinctive polygonal shape, it offers breathtaking views of the surroundings.

During the Middle Ages, Orford Castle was crucial to the protection of England's east coast. In addition to taking in the gorgeous surroundings, visitors may tour the museum and discover its history.

3. Beach and Heath Dunwich

A historical and environmental landmark is Dunwich Heath. The medieval town of Dunwich, which was once situated here on the Suffolk coast, has since been destroyed by coastal erosion. The heath is now a well-liked location for walking and birdwatching, as well as a refuge for wildlife.

Wander around the heath's pathways and take in the North Sea vistas. The National Trust oversees the property and offers details on the ecology and history of the region.

4. Iken's St. Botolph's Church

One of the oldest churches in Suffolk is St. Botolph's Church in Iken, which dates to the 7th century. The early Christian saint, St. Botolph, is said to have founded a monastery there. With a thatched roof and a little bell tower, the church exudes a straightforward, rustic charm.

The church's history and its role in the early spread of Christianity in England are available for visitors to learn about. The church's setting, with a view of the Alde Estuary, contributes to its tranquil ambiance.

5. The Abbey of Leiston
Near the town of Leiston is a ruined medieval abbey called Leiston Abbey. Augustinian monks lived in the abbey, which dates back to the 12th century. With its characteristic brickwork and stone arches, the abbey's remnants offer a glimpse into its former grandeur despite being partially destroyed.

Explore the grounds of the abbey and discover more about the monastic life that was once thriving here. During the summer, the location is often utilized for outdoor events and performances.

Conclusion

Suffolk is a county rich in history and cultural heritage, providing a broad assortment of notable monuments and historical places. From the prehistoric burial mounds at Sutton Hoo to the medieval castles and abbeys, there is something for everyone interested in discovering England's history. Whether you are attracted to the magnificent seaside cities or the lovely medieval villages, Suffolk promises a unique trip through time and culture.

CHAPTER FOUR: OUTDOOR ACTIVITIES AND NATURE

Suffolk's Natural Landscapes

The natural settings of Suffolk provide a rich and diverse atmosphere with plenty of chances for outdoor recreation. Let's investigate some of the most noteworthy natural features in the county.

The Area of Outstanding Natural Beauty (AONB) for the Suffolk Coast and Heaths AONB Suffolk Coast and Heaths covers an area of 155 square miles with a variety of ecosystems, such as forests, heathlands, shingle beaches, and salt marshes. It provides a distinctive combination of coastal and interior scenery and runs from the Stour Estuary in the south to Kessingland in the north.

Key Points: RSPB Minsmere is a well-known nature reserve that is home to many different bird species, such as marsh harriers, bitterns, and avocets. It offers great opportunities for birding with its network of paths and hides.

Dunwich Heath: A coastal heathland overseen by the National Trust, Dunwich Heath provides expansive vistas of the North Sea as well as a vibrant display of heather in late summer. It's a great place to hike and see nature.

Aldeburgh and Thorpeness: These seaside communities have shingle beaches and are excellent starting locations for excursions along the coast. The region provides a distinctive fusion of culture and environment and is rich in history.

Area of Outstanding Natural Beauty (AONB) in Dedham Vale

The scenic Dedham Vale and Stour Valley are included in the Dedham Vale AONB, which is located on the boundary between Suffolk and Essex. The landscape paintings of renowned painter

John Constable were influenced by the grandeur of this region.

Important Points of Interest: Flatford: This ancient community is the site of Flatford Mill, which became famous when Constable painted "The Hay Wain." There is a network of paths in the surrounding area that let people explore the scenes that influenced the artist.

Dedham: Another quaint town in the AONB, Dedham has boating and rowing access to the River Stour. With its old houses and art galleries, the village itself is a pleasure to explore.

The Stour Valley: This place is perfect for leisurely hikes and cycling due to its moderate hills and flowing river. There is a lot of wildlife in the region; otters and kingfishers may often be seen along the riverbanks.

The Brecks

The Brecks are a distinctive region northwest of Suffolk that is made up of large pine woods, heathlands, and sandy soils. It is renowned for its unique flora and wildlife and encompasses portions of Norfolk and Suffolk.

Key Features: Thetford Forest: With an extensive network of paths for hiking, cycling, and horseback riding, Thetford Forest is the biggest lowland pine forest in the United Kingdom. A wide range of species, including deer and uncommon birds, may be found in the woodland.

Brandon Country Park: This historic park, which is part of Thetford Forest, has a Victorian arboretum, formal gardens, and a number of walking routes. It's a well-liked family destination with a visitor center that provides details on the history and fauna of the park.

Santon Downham: Several riverside routes along the Little Ouse River are accessible from this settlement on the outskirts of Thetford Forest.

There are canoeing and kayaking options in this calm location.

Best Hiking and Walking Trails
The varied topography of Suffolk offers a multitude of hiking and walking routes. These are a few of the county's top trails, providing a variety of activities from forest treks to walks along the shore.

The Suffolk Coast Path
The Suffolk Coast Path is a 50-mile-long coastal route that stretches from Felixstowe in the south to Lowestoft in the north along the Suffolk coastline. Along with lovely seaside towns and villages, this walk provides a variety of coastal landscapes, including beaches, cliffs, and estuaries.

Principal Attractions: Orford to Aldeburgh: This route segment provides an attractive stroll beside the River Ore and the shore. You'll pass the charming village of Aldeburgh, the fascinating shingle spit with a military past, and Orford Ness National Nature Reserve along the route.

Southwold to Walberswick: This section links the charming hamlet of Walberswick with the beach resort of Southwold by means of a footbridge that spans the River Blyth. The walk offers breathtaking views of the coastline and wetlands, and the region is abundant in birds.

Lowestoft to Kessingland: This trail's northernmost stretch offers stunning views of the North Sea as it winds along beaches and cliffs. This stroll is made even more special by the fact that Lowestoft is the farthest easterly location in the United Kingdom.

The Path of Sandlings
The Sandlings Walk is a 60-mile-long path that connects Southwold and Ipswich, traveling through some of the most famous locations in Suffolk, such as Rendlesham Forest and Dunwich Heath. For

those who want a combination of forest and ocean vistas, this walk is perfect.

Highlights: Dunwich to Westleton: This stretch of the Sandlings Walk passes through the picturesque hamlet of Westleton and onto Dunwich Heath. When the heather is in full bloom in the late summer, it's an excellent way to view animals.

Rendlesham Forest: Hiking and cycling are popular outdoor activities in Rendlesham Forest, which this section of the path travels through. The hike is made more intriguing by the forest's reputation for seeing UFOs.

Levington to Ipswich: The Sandlings Walk's last section leads you into Ipswich by way of the River Orwell. The path offers a picturesque approach to the county town as well as views of the Orwell Bridge.

Trails of Ickworth House and Estate

Within its vast parkland and forest, Ickworth House, a National Trust site in Bury St. Edmunds, has a number of walking routes. Families and anyone seeking a more leisurely stroll may find these pathways suitable.

The Italianate Garden is one of the garden's main highlights. It is a formal space with a range of flowers and geometric patterns that make for a nice stroll. It's next to the striking Ickworth Rotunda, a distinctive architectural element.

The Trim Trail: Traveling through wide fields and forests, this 2.5-mile circle passes past the Ickworth Estate. The route has a number of training stations that make the stroll more enjoyable and engaging.

The Albana Wood Route: For people who like taking nature hikes, this woodland route is a fantastic choice. It passes through old-growth forests and provides views of deer and other animals, as well as a variety of bird species.

The method of Boudicca
The medieval town of Bury St Edmunds in Suffolk is 36 miles away from Diss in Norfolk along the Boudicca Way long-distance path. This path, named after the fabled queen Boudicca, travels among historic monuments and rural landscapes on old roads.

Highlights: Diss to Thetford: This route segment provides an insight into rural life as it winds through tiny communities and countryside. With its medieval castle mound and museum, the historic market town of Thetford is an excellent site to stop and explore.

From Thetford to Bury St. Edmunds: This section of the route passes through the center of Thetford Forest and into Bury St. Edmunds, a medieval town. The walk includes a variety of open and wooded areas, making it a worthwhile experience.

The Stour Valley Path

The Stour Valley Path is a 60-mile-long route that runs beside the River Stour from Cattawade, Suffolk, to Newmarket, Cambridgeshire. This path offers a chance to visit the Dedham Vale AONB while seeing the picturesque Stour Valley.

Key Highlights: Sudbury to Dedham: This path segment passes through the charming Dedham Vale, which is known for its flowing river and mild hills. The route goes past a number of quaint communities, such as Stratford St. Mary and Dedham.

Cattawade to Manningtree: The route ends at the Stour Estuary, which is the point where the river empties into the North Sea. Along with providing chances for photography and birding, the walk gives breathtaking views of the estuary.

Bures to Sudbury: The path travels through the rural areas around Bures and Sudbury in this segment. It makes for a serene and beautiful stroll as it winds through open meadows and forests.

CHAPTER FIVE: SUFFOLK'S COASTAL ATTRACTIONS

Beaches and Seaside Towns

The coastline of Suffolk is home to a wide variety of beaches, each providing a distinctive experience. There's a beach for everyone, whether it's shingle or sandy. Let's take a look at some of Suffolk's most well-liked coastal towns and beaches.

Aldeburgh

Situated along the Suffolk coast, Aldeburgh is a classic coastal town with miles of shingle beaches. Famous for its colorful arts scene, old-world architecture, and fresh seafood, Aldeburgh draws visitors looking for a classic coastal experience. The town is the site of the yearly Aldeburgh Festival, which honors music and the arts. Wander down the main street's many stores, galleries, and eateries, or take a leisurely stroll along the beach to see the vibrant fishermen's huts.

Beach Aldeburgh
Shingle beach Aldeburgh Beach offers stunning views of the North Sea. The beach is well-known for its distinctive scallop sculpture, which was made by artist Maggi Hambling as a tribute to the town's well-known composer, Benjamin Britten. In addition to taking leisurely strolls and beachcombing, beachgoers may take in the local fishermen at work. Seafood from the nearby vendors, particularly fish and chips, is another reason why people frequent the beach.

Southwold
The quaint coastal hamlet of Southwold has colorful beach cottages, a classic pier, and a sandy beach. A popular location for children and couples looking for a peaceful beach escape, Southwold is

well-known for its Victorian architecture and the famous Adnams Brewery.

Beach at Southwold

There is plenty of room on the sandy Southwold Beach for beach activities, including games and sunbathing. The scene is given a nostalgic feel by the ancient beach houses that border the shore. A variety of activities may be found at the historic Southwold Pier, which also has shops, arcades, and a café with expansive views of the coast. A promenade stroll or an exploration of the neighboring Southwold Harbour are further options for visitors.

Lowestoft

The northernmost coastal town in Suffolk, Lowestoft, is renowned for its vibrant beachfront, gorgeous sandy beaches, and extensive maritime heritage. The town is a well-liked family vacation spot because of its array of activities.

Beach Lowestoft

A broad sandy beach with shallow seas, Lowestoft Beach, often called South Beach, is perfect for swimming and water sports. The beach has a number of facilities, such as kid-friendly play areas, lifeguards, and beach houses. The yearly Lowestoft Air Show, which draws guests from all over the area, is also held at Lowestoft Beach. There are several entertainment choices available on the town's seaside, which is home to classic amusements, cafés, and stores.

Dunwich

The little community of Dunwich has a distinctive beach and a fascinating past. Due to coastal erosion, the once-bustling medieval town of Dunwich has almost vanished under the sea. With a combination of shingle and sandy beaches, it provides a serene and picturesque environment today.

Dunwich Shore

For those looking for a quiet getaway, Dunwich Beach is ideal since it is less congested and calmer. Surrounded by the stunning scenery of the Heaths Area of Outstanding Natural Beauty and the Suffolk Coast, the beach has a mixture of sand and shingle. Nearby Dunwich Heath is a National Trust site with walking paths and breathtaking coastal vistas that visitors may explore.

Thorpeness

The unusual coastal community of Thorpeness is well-known for its charming Meare (a man-made boating lake) and peculiar architecture. The town draws tourists who like discovering its peculiar features because of its special fairytale appeal.

Beach Thorpeness

A serene beach for a day along the seaside is Thorpeness Beach, which has pebbles. The beach is perfect for strolling, beachcombing, and taking in the North Sea vistas. Also accessible is Thorpeness Meare, a boating lake that drew inspiration from J.M. Barrie's "Peter Pan." Boating and paddleboarding are two of the water-based activities available at The Meare.

Felixstowe
Felixstowe is a lively coastal town that combines contemporary conveniences with period charm. The town is well-known for its long beaches, interesting waterfront, and historical sites.

Felixstowe Beach
North Beach and South Beach are two distinct areas of the long, sandy, shingle beach that makes up Felixstowe Beach. With its array of activities, including cafés, a seafront promenade, and amusement arcades, South Beach is a well-liked destination for families. For those looking for a more laid-back vibe, North Beach is calmer and perfect. Felixstowe Beach is an excellent spot for

water activities such as sailing, windsurfing, and kiteboarding.

Water Sports and Coastal Activities
Water sports and seaside activities abound throughout Suffolk's coastline, appealing to novices as well as seasoned aficionados. Listed here are a few of the most well-liked water sports and pastimes on the Suffolk coast.

Boating and sailing
The coast of Suffolk offers great sailing and boating conditions, with several marinas and sailing clubs situated along the beach. Popular sailing destinations include:

Orford: A bustling sailing community resides in this ancient hamlet. Sailing and boating in a picturesque environment are possible on the River Ore and the neighboring Orford Ness.

Woodbridge: Situated by the River Deben, Woodbridge is the home of the Woodbridge Cruising Club and hosts a number of annual boating and sailing events.

Thorpeness Meare: With rowboat and paddleboat rentals available, this artificial lake in Thorpeness is ideal for families and novice boaters.

Kiteboarding and windsurfing

Suffolk is a great place to windsurf and kiteboard because of its windy coastline. Some popular locations for these sports are:

Lowestoft: Lowestoft Beach is a well-liked windsurfing and kiteboarding location due to its shallow seas and steady winds.

Felixstowe: Kiteboarders and windsurfers are drawn to Felixstowe's North Beach due to the area's consistent high winds. Lessons and equipment rentals are provided by a number of schools and rental stores.

Southwold: This is another great spot for windsurfing and kiteboarding because of its sandy coastline and consistent winds.

Having a surf

Although Suffolk isn't well-known for its massive waves, it does have a few locations where surfing is feasible.

Southwold: Beginner surfers may sometimes find tiny waves at Southwold Beach. Because of its sandy bottom, the beach is a safe place to practice surfing.
Lowestoft: Another alternative for beginning surfers is Lowestoft's South Beach, which sometimes gets tiny waves.

Kayaking and paddleboarding

Along the Suffolk coast, paddleboarding and kayaking are popular sports that provide a leisurely opportunity to explore the rivers and shoreline. Popular venues for these kinds of events include:

River Deben: Paddleboarding and kayaking are great on the River Deben because of its serene waters and beautiful surroundings. Waldringfield and Woodbridge are well-liked starting locations.

Thorpeness Meare: Paddleboarding and kayaking are safe and enjoyable family activities on the man-made lake at Thorpeness.

Southwold: Those who want to explore the coastline from the ocean may go kayaking and paddleboarding along Southwold Beach.

Angling

There are chances for both river and sea fishing along the Suffolk coast, making fishing a classic pastime. Among the well-liked spots for fishing are:

Aldeburgh Beach: Fishermen may catch cod, bass, and whiting on this shingle beach, which is a well-liked location for sea fishing.

Orford Ness: With access to deeper waters and a variety of fish species, the secluded shingle spit of Orford Ness provides exceptional fishing chances.

Southwold Pier: With its authorized fishing grounds and breathtaking views of the coast, the pier at Southwold is a well-liked spot for recreational fishing.

Nature Trails and Coastal Walks

The coastline of Suffolk is home to many nature reserves and walking routes. It is a component of the Suffolk Coast and Heaths Area of Outstanding Natural Beauty. Typical hikes and routes along the seaside include:

Suffolk Coast Path: Encompassing the whole Suffolk coastline, the Suffolk Coast Path is a 50-mile-long route. It travels through a number of seaside communities and natural areas, offering breathtaking vistas and chances to see the local fauna.

Dunwich Heath: Dunwich Heath is a National Trust property with panoramic views of the coast and walking routes winding across heathland.

RSPB Minsmere: This nature reserve on the Suffolk coast has walking paths that go through a variety of ecosystems and is a great place to go birding.

In summary

Visitors of all ages and interests may enjoy a variety of activities at Suffolk's seaside attractions. There's something for everyone, from the shingle coastlines of Aldeburgh and Dunwich to the sandy beaches of Southwold and Lowestoft. Suffolk's coastline provides a wide variety of activities and places to explore, whether you're interested in water sports, coastal hikes, or seeing classic seaside villages.

CHAPTER SIX: ARTS AND CULTURE IN SUFFOLK

Museums, Theaters, and Galleries

Suffolk's museums

There are several museums in Suffolk that serve a variety of interests, including natural history, agriculture, and maritime history. Here are a few of the most well-known ones:

1. The Museum of Ipswich

One of Suffolk's most well-known museums is the Ipswich Museum. It has an extensive collection of human and natural history items, including a woolly mammoth, Egyptian mummies, and a Victorian natural history exhibit. It also looks at Ipswich's and the neighboring regions' local histories.

2. The East Anglian Life Museum

This outdoor museum, which is situated in Stowmarket, examines rural life in East Anglia. It has more than fifteen historic structures, such as farmhouses, a blacksmith's forge, and a watermill. The museum offers visitors an authentic experience of Suffolk's agricultural history via seasonal events and traditional craft activities.

3. The Sutton Hoo

A ship burial from the seventh century was found at the important Anglo-Saxon archaeological site of Sutton Hoo, which is close to Woodbridge. The location has a tourist center with displays on the history and relics of the Anglo-Saxons, which include a replica of the well-known helmet. Additional historical context for the burial mounds may be gained by taking a guided tour.

4. Museum Aldeburgh

The Tudor Moot Hall in Aldeburgh serves as the home of this museum. With displays on fishing, shipbuilding, and the town's historic architecture, it concentrates on the marine heritage of the area. Explore the influence of well-known people, including composer Benjamin Britten, who was closely associated with Aldeburgh.

5. The Heritage Centre at Long Melford
The Long Melford Heritage Centre delves into the town's past, highlighting its significance in the wool trade and its association with illustrious individuals such as Sir William Cordell. The center features historical records and regional items that provide insight into the town's history.

Suffolk theaters
The theatrical culture in Suffolk is rather active, with locations ranging from contemporary performance spaces to ancient playhouses. Some of Suffolk's most renowned theaters are as follows:

1. Wolsey Theatre, a new venue

The New Wolsey Theatre, a renowned regional theater with a location in Ipswich, is renowned for its varied programming. It presents a variety of family-friendly, comedic, dramatic, and musical performances. Through its innovative outreach and education initiatives, the theater is dedicated to fostering the growth of up-and-coming talent.

The Royal Theatre in Bury St. Edmunds

The Theatre Royal Bury St Edmunds is a historic venue with distinctive Georgian architecture, and it's the third-oldest functioning theater in the United Kingdom. It offers a variety of shows with a community emphasis, modern pieces, and classic plays. The rich history of the theater is shown via its legacy and guided tours.

3. The Theater at Quay

The Quay Theatre, a small theater in Sudbury, is the site of a range of events, such as live music, comedy, drama, and movie screenings. It is renowned for emphasizing the community and helping out regional artists and entertainers.

4. The Pavilion for Spas

The Spa Pavilion in Felixstowe provides a variety of entertainment, including live music, dancing, comedy, and theatrical shows. Its waterfront setting affords breathtaking vistas, and both local and visiting performances often use the theater as a venue.

5. Angles in the East

Ipswich is home to the traveling theatrical troupe Eastern Angles. It specializes in producing and presenting brand-new works that draw inspiration from East Anglia's rich cultural heritage. The group engages audiences around the area with performances that often explore regional themes and tales.

Suffolk Art Galleries
There are several art galleries in Suffolk that display both classic and modern pieces. Here are a few of the most important galleries to visit:

1. Gallery at Ipswich Art School
As a member of the Ipswich Museums and Galleries organization, the Ipswich Art School Gallery presents both classic and modern art on a temporary basis. The gallery offers a varied and constantly evolving selection of art to examine, including pieces by regional artists and traveling shows.

2. Gallery Artspace
The lively Artspace Gallery is a modern art gallery situated in Woodbridge. It features artwork from many different mediums, such as jewelry, pottery,

sculpture, and painting. The gallery is renowned for its ongoing, community-focused activities and workshops.

3. Gallery of the Fisher Theatre
There is a modest but notable gallery space within the Fisher Theatre in Bungay, where local artists have recurring shows. The gallery gives both known and up-and-coming artists a place to display their work to a larger audience.

4. The Gallery at Quay
The Quay Gallery, housed within the Quay Theatre in Sudbury, hosts exhibits of modern artwork created by local artists. It is an exciting venue that often hosts art exhibits that relate to the subjects of the plays to enhance the theater's programming.

5. Gallery Halesworth
This Halesworth gallery features a diverse range of art genres, including textiles, sculpture, painting,

and photography, and it has a strong community emphasis. Volunteers manage the gallery, which is dedicated to assisting regional creatives and artists.

Suffolk's Festivals and Events in 2024
Suffolk is well-known for its vibrant festivals and events, covering a broad spectrum of subjects like literature, music, art, and culture. A preview of some of the major celebrations and activities planned for 2024 is shown below:

1. The Aldeburgh Festival
Benjamin Britten, the composer, organized the famous classical music event, the Aldeburgh event, which takes place in the seaside town of Aldeburgh. A variety of symphonic performances, chamber music, opera, and contemporary pieces are presented throughout the festival. Bringing in world-class performers and groups, it's one of Suffolk's most important cultural gatherings.

2. Festival latitude

One of the most well-known music and arts events in the UK is the Latitude Festival, which takes place at Henham Park. It has a varied schedule of spoken word, theatrical, comedy, and musical acts. The event is renowned for its distinctive location, which has stages situated around scenic lakesides and woods. Latitude is kid-friendly as well, with kid-only spaces and activities.

3. IPA (Ipswich Arts Festival)

Every year, the Ipswich Arts Festival, often known as Ip-art, is a celebration of all types of art. The festival offers literary activities, theatrical shows, film screenings, music performances, and art exhibits. Its goals are to provide the Ipswich community with a diverse variety of cultural activities and to highlight local talent.

4. Suffolk Exhibition

Held in Trinity Park in Ipswich, the Suffolk Show is the county's biggest festival, centered on agriculture and the countryside. With cattle exhibits, equestrian activities, traditional crafts, and regional cuisine and drink, it honors Suffolk's rural past. A range of entertainment choices are also available during the exhibition, including family-friendly activities and live music.

5. Book Festival in Felixstowe

A literary festival, the Felixstowe Book Festival brings together Suffolk-based writers, publishers, and readers. It includes panel discussions, seminars, book signings, and author lectures. The festival honors literature and storytelling, with an emphasis on helping up-and-coming local and international writers.

6. The Maverick Festival

Held at Easton Farm Park, the Maverick Festival is a special occasion honoring American roots music.

With performers from both sides of the Atlantic, it offers a variety of performances in the genres of Americana, folk, country, and blues. The event provides a laid-back and personal setting where attendees may mingle with artists and take part in seminars.

7. Carnival at Beccles

Beccles Carnival is a well-known local celebration that includes a colorful procession, live music, and a carnival. For many years, the carnival has been a mainstay of the town's calendar, bringing visitors from all around Suffolk. It honors inventiveness and a sense of community.

In summary

Every passion may be satisfied by the diverse and vibrant arts and cultural scene that Suffolk has to offer. The county offers both locals and tourists a multitude of activities, from its bustling festivals and events to its historic museums and theaters. Suffolk offers a lot in 2024 and beyond, whether your interests are in taking in live concerts, learning about local history, or experiencing the festival atmosphere.

CHAPTER SEVEN: FOOD AND DRINK

Traditional Suffolk Cuisine

Suffolk's agricultural past and closeness to the North Sea are major influences on the region's traditional food. The county is renowned for its fresh seafood, products of the highest quality, and distinctive regional delicacies.

Ham from Suffolk

A popular local delicacy, Suffolk ham has a unique and delicious taste. Traditionally, it is produced from pigs raised in the rural areas of Suffolk, which are renowned for their superior meat. To preserve its moisture, the ham is cooked gently after being cured with a mixture of spices and salt. It is often served as part of a ploughman's meal, together with chutneys and mustard.

Faggots of Suffolk

Traditional British fare, pig offal, is used to make meatballs called 'faggots,' which are combined with breadcrumbs, onions, and spices. Faggots are often served with peas, mashed potatoes, and gravy in Suffolk. This meal, which has its origins in working-class neighborhoods, is still a comforting mainstay.

Cooking in Suffolk

A substantial meal like Suffolk stew is cooked using beef or lamb that is locally produced, along with a variety of vegetables, including potatoes, carrots, and turnips. The stew is cooked gently so that the flavors may combine to produce a filling and delicious dish. To help sop up the rich soup, crusty bread is often served with it.

Rusks of Suffolk

A sort of hard, dry biscuit prepared with flour, butter, and sugar is called a Suffolk rusk. Their texture makes them ideal for dipping, and they are usually consumed with tea or coffee. A classic Suffolk delight, rusks may be eaten as an easy snack or as a main course.

Seafood Appetizers

The coastal location of Suffolk means that fresh fish is plentiful. Common mainstays in the local cuisine include mussels from the River Blyth, oysters from the Deben, and a variety of seafood from the North Sea. A British staple, fish and chips are especially well-liked in Suffolk, where they're often served with mushy peas on the side.

Suffolk Cheddar

The history of manufacturing cheese in Suffolk is growing, with several artisanal cheesemakers creating distinctive kinds. The semi-hard cow's milk cheese, Suffolk Gold, is prized for its rich taste and creamy texture. Another well-liked cheese is Baron

Bigod, a raw milk cheese with a national reputation similar to Brie.

Best Restaurants and Pubs to Visit
Suffolk is home to a diverse selection of eateries, ranging from quaint rural pubs to Michelin-starred restaurants. These are a few of the top spots to check out the local food and beverage scene.

The Raucous Hound, Bromeswell
The multi-award-winning gastropub, The Unruly Pig, is renowned for its creative take on traditional British fare. This tavern, which is close to Woodbridge, a market town, has a seasonal cuisine with products that are obtained locally. The Unruly Pig is popular among both residents and tourists because its meals often combine classic British ingredients with modern cooking methods.

Lavenham's Swan

In the ancient town of Lavenham, there's a historic hotel and restaurant called The Swan. The restaurant emphasizes using food that is produced locally and delivers a variety of classic British cuisine with a contemporary touch. The dining area at The Swan is tastefully furnished, providing a classy atmosphere for a special dinner. A well-known feature of the hotel's bar is its assortment of premium wines and spirits.

Stanton's Leaping Hare
Unique dining establishment The Leaping Hare is located in Wyken Vineyards, close to Bury St. Edmunds. Fresh, in-season foods are included in the restaurant's cuisine, which draws inspiration from the nearby farm and vineyards. While dining, guests may take in views of the vineyard and savor delicacies like roasted Suffolk lamb and seafood that is produced locally. Additionally, there is a wine store at The Leaping Hare that sells wines made on the property.

The Aldeburgh Brudenell

In the beach town of Aldeburgh, there is a restaurant called The Brudenell that has breathtaking views of the North Sea. The menu features pan-seared scallops and grilled lobster, two of the greatest seafood delicacies from Suffolk. During the warmer months, diners love to enjoy alfresco dining on the Brudenell's outside patio, where they can take in the sea air.

The Crown, Southwold

Known for its connection to Adnams Brewery, The Crown is a classic bar in the quaint village of Southwold. This pub serves substantial pies and fish & chips, among other traditional pub cuisine, and has a cozy, welcoming ambiance. Adnams beers and ales, which are made just a short distance away, are also available in large quantities at The Crown.

Ipswich's Greyhound

In the center of Ipswich, The Greyhound is a bustling bar renowned for its varied cuisine and friendly ambiance. The menu at the pub is diverse, ranging from classic British meals to more modern selections. The Greyhound routinely holds live music and events, and its beer garden is a well-liked location for alfresco eating.

Kesgrave Hall, Milsom's Kesgrave

Situated in a stunning country mansion close to Ipswich, Milsom's Kesgrave Hall is a chic hotel and restaurant. The eatery serves contemporary British cuisine with a focus on foods that are obtained locally. Foods like roasted chicken and slow-cooked pork belly are served to guests in a classy but laid-back atmosphere. During the summer, the outside patio makes a beautiful background for eating al fresco.

The Ship in Dunwich

The Ship at Dunwich is a quaint bar situated in the seaside community of Dunwich, which is well-known for its picturesque surroundings and extensive history. The tavern has a cuisine that highlights locally produced, fresh seafood, including grilled mackerel and fish pie. The ship is a well-liked stop for tourists touring the region because of its close proximity to Dunwich Heath and Beach.

In summary

The culinary and beverage landscape of Suffolk is a fascinating mix of innovation and tradition. There is a wide variety of eating experiences to be had in the county's restaurants and pubs, but traditional Suffolk cuisine delivers filling and substantial meals. Suffolk has options for every taste, whether you're looking for a classy eating place, a cozy pub, or a restaurant by the sea. The culinary and beverage scene in Suffolk is certain to make an impact, with its emphasis on locally produced foods and friendly hospitality.

CHAPTER EIGHT: SHOPPING AND LOCAL PRODUCTS

Suffolk's Markets and Boutiques

Conventional Marketplaces

1. Market in Bury St. Edmunds

This ancient street market is situated in the center of Bury St. Edmunds, a historic town that has been around for almost a millennium. It is held every Wednesday and Saturday and has more than 80 vendors selling a wide range of products, such as baked foods, fresh fruit, meats, cheeses, apparel, crafts, and antiques. Local delicacies, including Suffolk pig and freshly picked vegetables from neighboring farms, are available to guests.

2. The Ipswich Market

The county town of Suffolk, Ipswich, has a thriving market in the Cornhill neighborhood. It offers a combination of classic and contemporary booths and is open four days a week. Fresh fish, handmade bread, confections, and locally roasted coffee are available to shoppers. The market serves as a social center for the neighborhood and offers plenty of chances to taste regional goods in a welcoming environment.

3. The market in Sudbury

The twice-weekly market in Sudbury is well-known for its fresh vegetables, plants, and handicrafts. The vibe of this market is quite rustic, evoking the surrounding countryside of the town. In addition to handcrafted jewelry and ceramics, local producers of cheeses, honey, and jams are available for purchase.

Handmade Stores

1. Snape Maltings

Situated on the River Alde, Snape Maltings is a unique location that has an array of small stores, galleries, and cafés. High-end, regionally produced goods, such as ceramics, textiles, and gourmet food items, are the focus of these shops. The Aldeburgh Festival is held there as well, which contributes to the area's vibrant cultural environment.

2. The Gift Shop at Lavenham Guildhall

One of the best-preserved medieval villages in England is Lavenham, and the town's ancient beauty is reflected in the Guildhall Gift Shop. A carefully chosen assortment of regional handicrafts, literature, and mementos that honor Lavenham's history may be found here for guests. Being a member of the National Trust guarantees a superior level of authenticity and quality.

3. Woodbridge's Main Road

In Woodbridge, The Thoroughfare is a busy road dotted with stand-alone stores and boutiques. There are shops here that sell gourmet foods, apparel, literature, antiques, and modern and classic shopping experiences. Known for their unique collections, two notable stores are Browsers Bookshop and Woodbridge Antiques Centre.

Modern shopping malls

1. Ipswich's Buttermarket Shopping Center
The Buttermarket Shopping Centre, a contemporary shopping center featuring a range of high-street names and independent stores, is situated in the center of Ipswich. It incorporates local aspects while providing a more modern retail experience. A variety of apparel businesses, electronics merchants, and specialized cuisine establishments are available to visitors.

2. The Arc Shopping Center in Bury St. Edmunds

The Arc is a chic, contemporary Bury St. Edmunds retail mall. It offers a variety of shopping opportunities since it is home to both local shops and major businesses. The center's open-air layout and modern architecture are well-known for making guests feel comfortable.

Unique Souvenirs from Suffolk

Specialties in Food and Drink:

1. Suffolk Cider

Cider is a popular commodity in Suffolk, where there are several cideries and orchards spread out over the county. Based in Suffolk, Aspall is one of the UK's oldest cider manufacturers, with a variety of tastes ranging from traditional apple to more daring. Gift sets or bottles are available for purchase, making them perfect keepsakes.

2. Honey from Suffolk

There are several beekeepers in Suffolk that produce honey of excellent quality. Markets and farm stores sell local honey, which is often available in a range of flavors based on the flowers the bees have visited. This creates a tasty and distinctive memento that embodies the natural beauty of Suffolk.

3. Smoked fish from Aldeburgh

Aldeburgh is a seaside town well-known for its smoked fish, especially its smoked salmon and kippers. These treats are available to tourists in neighborhood markets and fishmongers; they are often packed for convenient travel. For those who like fish, it's a pleasant memento of Suffolk's maritime past.

Handicrafts and handmade items

1. Pottery in Suffolk

The pottery sector in Suffolk is flourishing, with regional artists producing exquisite ceramic objects. These include ornamental vases and sculptures, as well as practical objects like bowls and mugs. These one-of-a-kind sculptures, which uniquely capture the essence of the county and the artist's flair, are sold in boutiques and galleries around the county.

2. Articles Made of Wool
Wool manufacturing has a long history in Suffolk, and local artists are still producing high-quality textiles to carry on this legacy. Woolen scarves, blankets, and knitted items are available for purchase at a variety of boutiques and craft stores. These products are fashionable and useful mementos, as they often include natural fabrics and traditional designs.

3. Photography and artwork in Suffolk
Numerous painters and photographers have drawn inspiration from the county's scenic landscapes and

historic villages. Suffolk's natural beauty is captured in the original paintings, prints, and photos that are sold in local galleries and stores. These items provide distinctive mementos that provide enduring recollections of a trip to the county.

Customized Items and Crafts

1. The Suffolk Lace
There is a centuries-old lace-making history in Suffolk. Local artists still practice this technique today, producing elaborate lace goods like tablecloths, handkerchiefs, and doilies. These elegant items provide a lasting memento and pay homage to Suffolk's heritage and workmanship.

2. Woodwork in Suffolk
Suffolk is renowned for its woodworking heritage, with regional artisans producing one-of-a-kind wooden items, furniture, and sculptures. A variety of wooden goods, ranging in size from modest

décor pieces to substantial furniture, are available for visitors to see, all of which highlight the talent and creativity of Suffolk's woodworkers.

3. Exceptional presents from Suffolk
Unique items may be found all around the area, since Suffolk is a county that cherishes its history and customs. When it comes to picking out unique keepsakes, tourists to Suffolk are spoilt for choice. Some examples of such items are a finely woven woolen scarf, a bottle of locally produced cider, and handcrafted pottery. These items capture the spirit of Suffolk, making them ideal as presents or as a keepsake of a trip to this enchanting county.

In conclusion, there is a wide variety of shopping experiences available in Suffolk, ranging from modern malls to traditional marketplaces, artisan boutiques to heritage-based gift stores. Suffolk offers a variety of unique mementos that are both memorable and unusual, reflecting the county's rich history, cultural heritage, and dedication to workmanship. Suffolk has something for everyone, regardless of their interests—foodies, crafters, or those looking for unusual presents.

CHAPTER NINE: ACCOMMODATION IN SUFFOLK

Hotels, Inns, and B&Bs

Suffolk hotels

There is a wide range of hotels in Suffolk, from high-end boutique properties to well-known franchises. Here are a few of the top choices:

1. Lavenham's Swan Hotel

Situated in the ancient town of Lavenham, the Swan establishment is an opulent establishment dating back to the 15th century. Reputable for its warm ambience and timber-framed construction, this establishment has tastefully furnished rooms, a spa, and a fine dining restaurant. For those looking for a romantic or historic environment, this is an excellent option.

2. Aldeburgh's Brudenell Hotel

The four-star Brudenell Hotel in Aldeburgh is located on the waterfront and offers breathtaking views of the ocean. In addition to having contemporary, cozy rooms, the hotel has a well-liked seafood restaurant. For beach lovers and those who like to visit the Heaths Area of Outstanding Natural Beauty and the Suffolk Coast, this is the perfect place.

3. The Bury St. Edmunds Ickworth Hotel

The Ickworth Hotel is a family-friendly lodging located in an 18th-century house that is a part of the Ickworth House estate. It has large gardens, an indoor pool, and a range of kid-friendly activities. The hotel is a fantastic option for families since it combines opulence with kid-friendly services.

4. Southwold's Crown Hotel

The Crown Hotel is a boutique establishment with uniquely designed rooms and an award-winning restaurant, situated in the quaint seaside village of Southwold. It is well-known for its assortment of regional wines and ales and offers quick access to the famous Southwold Pier and the coastline.

The Bury St. Edmunds Hotel, The Angel Hotel
The Angel Hotel is a historic establishment in the center of Bury St. Edmunds that blends traditional elegance with contemporary amenities. Because of its position, you may easily visit the town's historic landmarks, such as the Theatre Royal and Bury St. Edmunds Abbey.

Suffolkn Inns
Inns in Suffolk, which are often found in picturesque rural locations, provide a more personal and traditional experience. The following are a few notable inns:

The vessel in Dunwich

Situated close to the Suffolk Coast in the little community of Dunwich, there is a classic inn called The Ship at Dunwich. With its exposed fireplaces and wooden beams, it has a rustic appeal. Visitors may take leisurely strolls along the shoreline and visit neighboring natural areas such as RSPB Minsmere.

2. Woolpit's Bull Inn

The 16th-century Bull Inn in Woolpit has a cozy, welcoming ambiance. It serves substantial meals and a variety of regional ales in a typical pub setting. It's a terrific starting point for exploring the local countryside since the accommodations are attractively designed and cozy.

3. Badingham's White Horse

The White Horse is a quaint inn in the town of Badingham that is well-known for its tasty meals and friendly staff. The inn offers visitors a tranquil environment with a garden and a comfortable parlor room.

4. Horringer's The Six Bells
The Horringer country inn, The Six Bells, is located close to Bury St. Edmunds. It has a typical pub with great food and a choice of well-appointed accommodations. It's a great option for anyone who wants to be near popular sights like Ickworth House while still having a rural getaway.

5. Snape's Crown Inn
Located in Snape Village, The Crown Inn is a classic inn with a contemporary flair. It is adjacent to Snape Maltings, a well-liked cultural attraction, and has cozy accommodations. Visitors may explore the neighboring natural areas and take in the local music scene.

Suffolk Bed & Breakfasts

In Suffolk, bed and breakfasts (B&Bs) provide a more individualized experience; they are often owned by local hosts who give insider information on things to do in the region. Among Suffolk's notable B&Bs are the following:

1. The Stowmarket Bays Farm
The opulent B&B Bays Farm is situated close to Stowmarket. Elegant rooms and well-planted grounds may be found in this exquisitely renovated 17th-century farmhouse. Visitors may unwind in the tranquil settings while savoring a substantial breakfast prepared with regional food.

2. Kettlebaston's Old Rectory
The Old Rectory is a quaint bed and breakfast located in Kettlebaston hamlet. This Georgian-style rectory has large rooms, a lovely garden, and serves a hearty English breakfast. It's a great starting point for seeing the medieval villages and rural areas of Suffolk.

3. Woodbridge's Colston Hall Farmhouse

Near Woodbridge is a family-run bed and breakfast called Colston Hall Farmhouse. This charming house is surrounded by a rural area and has cozy rooms. Known for their warm hospitality, the hosts serve out a delectable, prepared breakfast every morning to their visitors.

4. Tuddenham, Tuddenham Mill

Set in a renovated watermill, Tuddenham Mill is a unique bed and breakfast. It has a gourmet restaurant and chic accommodations with modern design features. With views of the nearby meadows and the millpond, the location is serene.

5. Lavenham's Great House

Lavenham's historic bed and breakfast, The Great House, has French-inspired décor. It has a well-regarded restaurant and opulent accommodations. For those looking for a classy, private encounter in a historic setting, our B&B is perfect.

Tips for Finding the Perfect Stay

The ideal place to stay in Suffolk will depend on a number of variables, such as your tastes, location, and budget. The following advice will assist you in selecting the ideal lodging option:

1. Establish your budget.

Determine your budget before looking for a place to stay. There are several alternatives available in Suffolk, ranging from opulent hotels to reasonably priced inns. You can make fewer decisions if you are aware of your budget.

2. Examine the place

Consider your lodging options in Suffolk. Think about visiting places like Southwold or Aldeburgh if you like beach activities. If you'd rather be in the country, try to find lodging close to Lavenham or

Bury St. Edmunds. Think about how close you are to eateries, transit, and activities.

3. Select the appropriate type of accommodation.

Choose the kind of lodging that best meets your needs. Hotels can be your best option if you want a full-service experience with restaurants and spas. Inns or B&Bs are good options if you want a more private, intimate atmosphere.

4. Examine ratings and reviews.

To learn more about the caliber of the lodging and the experiences of previous visitors, go through internet reviews and ratings. For this reason, websites like Booking.com and TripAdvisor are great tools. Examine reviews for recurring topics to determine the general quality of the lodging.

5. Seek out packages and special offers.

Particularly during off-peak seasons, a lot of hotels and inns offer exclusive packages or discounts. To take advantage of special offers and promotions, think about making your reservation straight via the hotel's website.

6. Find out about the facilities.
Consider the facilities that are essential to you. Look for lodgings with family-friendly amenities like playgrounds or swimming pools if you're traveling with kids. If you're organizing a romantic retreat, look for locations that offer great eating establishments or spas.

7. Review the policy on cancellations.
Take a look at the cancellation policy before booking. Being adaptable is crucial, particularly if your plans might alter. Select lodging that has a reasonable cancellation policy to steer clear of unforeseen costs.

8. Make direct contact with the accommodation.

If you have any special queries or demands, you may want to get in touch with the lodging directly. This may help you gauge their timeliness and quality of customer service. It's also an excellent time to find out about any needs or unique requests.

9. Take the weather and season into account.

The season has an effect on what you can do in Suffolk. The summer is the busiest and most costly travel season because of the nicer weather and more activities. A good mix of nice weather and fewer people may be found in the spring and fall. While it's calmer in the winter, certain attractions can have shortened hours.

10. Make a plan beforehand.

Popular spots in Suffolk tend to fill up fast, particularly during busy times of the year or important occasions. To guarantee your chosen lodging, make advance plans and reservations. You may also benefit from early booking savings by doing this.

You may find the ideal lodging in Suffolk with confidence for your next vacation if you keep these pointers in mind. Suffolk has a variety of choices to meet the demands of every tourist, whether they like the comfort of a bed and breakfast, the elegance of a historic hotel, or the charm of a classic inn.

CHAPTER TEN: CONCLUSION

Planning Your Trip to Suffolk

When to Go: Nestled in the eastern region of England, Suffolk provides a blend of scenic coasts, ancient towns, and rustic appeal. The ideal time to go will depend on your tastes. The summer months of June through August are the busiest travel times, offering pleasant weather, colorful festivals, and crowded beaches. Spring (March to May) and fall (September to November) bring with them warmer temperatures, fewer tourists, and picturesque scenery of blossoming flowers or changing foliage. Winter (December to February) is the best time to go if you want peace and cheaper lodging.

How to Travel There

You may get to Suffolk via a variety of transportation options. Norwich International and London Stansted are the closest airports. To get to Suffolk, you may take the train or hire a vehicle from these airports. Ipswich and Bury St. Edmunds are two important train terminals with connections to London and other UK towns. Major highways such as the A14 and A12 provide easy access to Suffolk's main locations if you'd rather drive.

Where to stay
There are many different lodging choices available in Suffolk, ranging from opulent hotels and quaint bed & breakfasts to self-catering cottages and campgrounds. Both contemporary hotels and old inns can be found in Ipswich. Charming boutique hotels and guesthouses with sea views may be found in coastal towns like Southwold and Aldeburgh. Staying in a country home or farm B&B in places like Framlingham or Lavenham may provide a more rustic experience.

How to Proceed

There are a wide variety of activities and attractions in Suffolk. The following suggestions are provided:

Visit Historic Towns: Lavenham, with its half-timbered buildings from the Middle Ages, and Bury St. Edmunds, with its magnificent cathedral and the remnants of an old monastery, are two places to visit. It's also worthwhile to explore Orford Castle and Framlingham Castle.

Visit the Coastline: miles of sandy beaches, quaint fishing towns, and nature reserves can be found along Suffolk's coastline. Popular beach towns include Southwold and Aldeburgh; for those who like the outdoors and birdwatching, Dunwich Heath and RSPB Minsmere are great locations.

Take in Local Culture: Attend one of Suffolk's numerous festivals, such as the comedy, art, and music-focused Latitude Festival or the classical music-focused Aldeburgh Festival. Additionally, Suffolk is well-known for its thriving culinary scene, which features regional products in gourmet restaurants and farmers' markets.

Outdoor Activities: Walking, cycling, and horseback riding are all excellent in Suffolk's rural areas. There are breathtaking vistas from the Suffolk Coast Path, and hiking and mountain biking are excellent in Thetford Forest.

What to Pack: Take into account the time of year and the activities you have scheduled. Bring light clothes, sunglasses, a hat, and sunscreen in the summer. Bring layers, a water-resistant jacket, and cozy walking shoes for the spring and fall. In the winter, pack warm clothes, a hat, gloves, and a scarf. To fully appreciate the beautiful splendor of Suffolk, a camera is a must.

Aspects of Safety and Health to Consider

Travelers may feel secure in Suffolk most of the time. But it's always a good idea to use basic prudence. Watch for your possessions, particularly in busy places, and don't leave valuables in your vehicle where they may be easily seen. Be mindful of the local animals and stick to established trails while visiting nature reserves or seaside regions. Make sure your travel insurance includes emergency medical coverage if you have any health problems.

Regional Traditions and Protocols

Suffolk's culture is courteous and restrained, much like that of the rest of England. When you go to small businesses, be patient and kind. In restaurants, tipping is expected (10–15% is typical), and it's considerate to express gratitude to employees for their assistance. A bottle of wine or a box of chocolates is a typical modest present to offer when you are welcomed to someone's house.

Final Thoughts and Recommendations

Suffolk is a mesmerizing location that provides a special fusion of local character, natural beauty, and history. Suffolk offers activities to suit all interests, including seeing historical sites, relaxing on the beach, and engaging in local culture. In order to maximize your experience, here are a few last suggestions:

Accept the culture of the place.

Suffolk is renowned for its vibrant cultural past and strong sense of community. To get a taste of real Suffolk life, go to farmers' markets, tour tiny towns, and attend local festivals. Talking to locals is encouraged since they are often eager to provide tips and anecdotes.

Take your time.

It is ideal to experience Suffolk slowly. Spend some time lounging on the beach, exploring the countryside, and strolling around old neighborhoods. In order to really enjoy the area's natural beauty, think about renting a bicycle or taking a stroll along some of the picturesque paths.

Find undiscovered treasures.
Although Suffolk is home to several well-known sites, there are a ton of undiscovered treasures there as well. Look for distinctive stores and cafés, explore rural regions, and visit lesser-known places. You will feel more connected to the area and its inhabitants if you use this method.

Encourage regional companies.
A large number of enterprises in Suffolk are run and owned individually. You'll boost the local economy and aid in maintaining the distinctive flavor of the region by patronizing neighborhood stores, eateries, and lodging facilities. Make an effort to purchase goods created locally and eat at family-run eateries.

Observe the environment.

One of Suffolk's most valuable assets is its natural beauty, which must be preserved. When visiting coastal regions or nature reserves, abide by responsible tourist rules. Be mindful of animals, respect designated trails, and refrain from littering. When visiting a beach, remember to pack up your garbage and think about joining in on beach clean-ups.

Make a weather plan.

Even in the summer, Suffolk's weather isn't always dependable. Carry an umbrella or waterproof jacket, and pack in layers in case the weather changes. In this manner, regardless of the weather, you'll be prepared to enjoy your vacation.

Make advance reservations.

Consider booking accommodations in advance if you're going during the busiest time of year or attending a well-attended event. This includes lodging, dining establishments, and attractions that require a ticket. You'll have an easier and more pleasurable vacation if you prepare beforehand.

Maintain an open mind.
With its ancient sites, contemporary conveniences, bucolic settings, and energetic coastal cities, Suffolk is a location of contrast. Accept variety and have an open mind to new things. There's always something new to explore, whether you're strolling around a historic castle, taking in some classical music, or watching the waves at the beach.

Suffolk provides a unique vacation experience by mixing culture, history, and the natural world. You will have an amazing and fulfilling vacation in this stunning area if you properly arrange your itinerary and heed our advice. Have fun while you're in Suffolk!

HAPPY TRAVELS!!!

Printed in Great Britain
by Amazon